BERLIN 2014

THE CITY AT A GLANCE

D1545565

Unter den Linden

Named after its sticky lime trees, the boulevard's attractions include the Stalinist Russian Embassy (No 63-65, T 229 1110), and the Empty Library at Bebelplatz, marking the spot where the Nazis burned books in 1933.

Gendarmenmarkt

Reworked by Georg Christian Unger in 1777, this 1688 square is Berlin's most spectacular. The site of the Konzerthaus (T 203 092 333), it also hosts a lively Christmas market.

Museumsinsel

Of the big five museums on this island in the Spree, the Pergamon (Bodestrasse 1-3, T 266 424 242) and David Chipperfield's renovated Neues Museum (see p069) are the standouts.

Fernsehturm

Now an iconic landmark, the TV Tower was finished in 1969. GDR leaders were dismayed to see that the sun's reflection off their 'ball on a spike' appeared as a giant crucifix.
See p015

Checkpoint Charlie

The main border crossing between East and West during the Cold War is now a rather embarrassing tourist circus, and it's hard to picture the tense stand-offs of the past.

GSW Headquarters

Sauerbruch Hutton's renovation of a 1950s office building is a beacon of urban renewal.
See p013

Karl-Marx-Allee

Although the shopping on this communist take on the Champs-Élysées may be lousy, the Kino International (see p064) and Café Moskau (No 34) are well worth a look.

INTRODUCTION
THE CHANGING FACE OF THE URBAN SCENE

Berlin is now firmly established as one of the world's great cultural capitals. What it lacks in financial clout, when compared with other big German cities such as Frankfurt or Munich, it compensates for with energy and creative buzz. Its art fairs and exhibitions, including the Berlin Biennale and ABC Art Berlin Contemporary, draw global attention, and Berlin Fashion Week is a key fixture in the style arena. In 2014, it will finally get a major airport suited to its status as the third most-visited city in Europe. But the sleek Brandenburg International has already been delayed three times, so locals will only believe it when they see it.

It is not unusual for a casual visitor to the city to end up as a permanent resident, and new Berliners abound, opening galleries, studios and shops in still-plentiful underused urban spaces. As a result of this influx, the cheap rents have started to climb, pushing the culture crowd into one upcoming area after another.

Famously, this is a city that never sleeps. During the days of the Weimar Republic, the capital gained a reputation as a hedonistic party town, and the label still applies today. From underground events to hardcore techno clubs, the nightlife is as diverse as the city. It may have its edgy moments, but Berlin is comparatively safe. It has a well-run municipal infrastructure, and even after burning the candle at both ends, you are never far from the familiar warmth of a custard-coloured taxi to whisk you home.

ESSENTIAL INFO
FACTS, FIGURES AND USEFUL ADDRESSES

TOURIST OFFICE
Berlin Tourist Information
Pariser Platz
T 250 025
www.visitberlin.de

TRANSPORT
Airport transfer to Mitte
JetExpressBus TXL
www.bvg.de
Buses depart regularly between 6am and
11pm. The journey takes 30 to 40 minutes
S-Bahn/U-Bahn
www.bvg.de
Trains run from 4am to 1am, Sunday to
Thursday; 24 hours, Fridays and Saturdays
Taxis
Funk Taxi Berlin
T 261 026
Cabs can also be hailed on the street
Travel card
A 72-hour WelcomeCard costs €24.50 and
includes discounts to many attractions

EMERGENCY SERVICES
Ambulance/Fire
T 112
Police
T 110
24-hour pharmacy
Apotheke Berlin Hauptbahnhof
T 2061 4190

EMBASSIES
British Embassy
Wilhelmstrasse 70
T 204 570
www.ukingermany.fco.gov.uk
US Embassy
Clayallee 170
T 8305 1200
germany.usembassy.gov

POSTAL SERVICES
Post office
Königstrasse 27/28
T 018 023 333
www.deutschepost.de
Shipping
UPS
T 018 0588 2663
www.ups.com

BOOKS
Berlin by Freunde von Freunden (Distanz)
Goodbye to Berlin
by Christopher Isherwood (Vintage)

WEBSITES
Architecture
www.german-architects.com
Art/Design
www.artnews.org
Newspaper
www.spiegel.de/international

EVENTS
Berlin Biennale
www.berlinbiennale.de
Berlin Fashion Week
www.fashion-week-berlin.com
International Film Festival
www.berlinale.de

COST OF LIVING
Taxi from Tegel Airport to Mitte
€27
Cappuccino
2.50
Packet of cigarettes
€5
Daily newspaper
€0.70
Bottle of champagne
€70

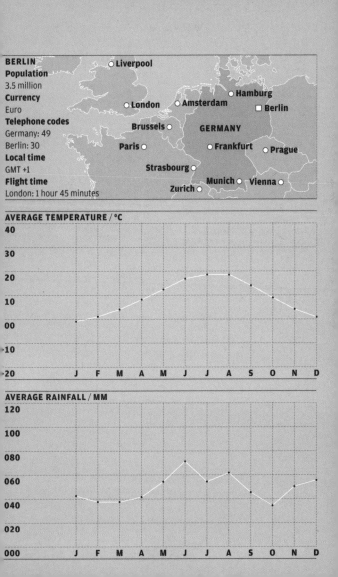

BERLIN
Population
3.5 million
Currency
Euro
Telephone codes
Germany: 49
Berlin: 30
Local time
GMT +1
Flight time
London: 1 hour 45 minutes

Liverpool

London Amsterdam Hamburg □ Berlin

Brussels **GERMANY**

Paris Frankfurt Prague

Strasbourg

Munich Vienna

Zurich

AVERAGE TEMPERATURE / °C

| | 40 | 30 | 20 | 10 | 00 | -10 | -20 |
| J F M A M J J A S O N D |

AVERAGE RAINFALL / MM

| 120 | 100 | 080 | 060 | 040 | 020 | 000 |
| J F M A M J J A S O N D |

NEIGHBOURHOODS
THE AREAS YOU NEED TO KNOW AND WHY

To help you navigate the city, we've chosen the most interesting districts (see below and the map inside the back cover) and colour-coded our featured venues, according to their location; those venues that are outside these areas are not coloured.

TIERGARTEN

Past the Brandenburg Gate, Tiergarten is home to the Reichstag (see p064) and the Haus der Kulturen der Welt (see p066), as well as modernist architectural gems by Oscar Niemeyer and Alvar Aalto in Hansaviertel. Further south, art galleries, such as Blain|Southern (Potsdamer Strasse 77-87, T 644 931 510), are commonplace.

SCHEUNENVIERTEL

Although it's touristy on the surface, Scheunenviertel's backstreets are packed with interesting boutiques, such as Objets Trouvés (see p073) and Apartment (see p085). In this area you'll find furniture and clothes by local designers, and big-label German stores like Hugo Boss and Adidas.

KREUZBERG

Once the hangout of left-wing punks and anarchists, Kreuzberg has transformed radically since reunification, but the area has kept its healthy cultural mix. During summer, it's a happy place to eat, chill out and socialise. A more sobering experience is the Jewish Museum (see p064).

FRIEDRICHSHAIN

First impressions tend to be of six-lane thoroughfares lined with epic communist-era architecture, and old stretches of the Wall covered in street art. But dive off into the side roads around Boxhagener Platz and you'll discover many cafés, bars, retro furniture shops and restaurants.

CHARLOTTENBURG

There's no question that Charlottenburg is a little duller for its gentrification, but Kurfürstendamm, the main shopping drag, is worth a look, and this area is where to stay for affordable luxury – at Hotel-Pension Dittberner (see p030), for example. Don't miss the Olympiastadion (see p089), built for the 1936 Games.

MITTE

The historic city çentre was the first district to be smartened up after the Wall came down. Now it is a dense mix of refurbished 18th- and 19th-century apartments, GDR *Plattenbauten* (prefabs) and new-builds. Modern architecture has sprung up in the derelict, war-torn gaps.

PRENZLAUER BERG

Many of the 19th-century houses in this once decaying working-class district have been spruced up and are now occupied by arty young families. The scene centres around Knaackstrasse and Kollwitzplatz. Lazy Sunday breakfasts are de rigueur, if the kids don't drive you to distraction.

SCHÖNEBERG

The verdant boroughs of former West Berlin are home to grand old hotels, and a cluster of contemporary art galleries, most of which are hidden in courtyards along Potsdamer Strasse. From here, it's only a 20-minute drive to the lakefront beaches of the Wannsee (see p100).

LANDMARKS
THE SHAPE OF THE CITY SKYLINE

The landmark most visitors want to see is the one that no longer exists: the Berlin Wall. Forget the touristy mock-up of the former Checkpoint Charlie on Friedrichstrasse, and instead head for the more poignant Berlin Wall Memorial along the southern side of Bernauer Strasse (www.berliner-mauer-gedenkstaette.de).

Just as the traces left by the Wall are increasingly hard to find, so are differences between 'East' and 'West' as the city expands into the gaps left by history. The stretch of New Internationalist and Stalinist architecture from Alexanderplatz down Karl-Marx-Allee is very 'East', but you will struggle to find any communist drabness in the renovated area it leads to around Oberbaum City (overleaf) and the cafés on Mainzer Strasse in Friedrichshain.

Despite having functioned as two cities for 41 years, Berlin is well signposted and has an efficient transport system. The only headache is the doubling up of buildings, such as opera houses Deutsche Oper in the West (Bismarckstrasse 35, T 343 8401) and Staatsoper – under renovation until 2014 – to the East (Unter den Linden 7, T 203 540), and conference centres ICC (see p012) and BCC (Alexanderstrasse 11, T 2380 6750). Confusion over the two mainline stations, Ostbahnhof and Bahnhof Zoologischer Garten, located in the East and West, was resolved with the 2006 opening of Meinhard von Gerkan's central Hauptbahnhof (Europaplatz). *For full addresses, see Resources.*

Narva-Turm

The brick building that housed the Narva light-bulb factory and test laboratory east of Warschauer Strasse was redeveloped into offices in 2000 as part of the revamp of the Oberbaum City area. A large glass cube was added to the top, which, when lit up at night, is a 63m-high beacon to those heading out for a night's partying in Friedrichshain or Kreuzberg.
Rotherstrasse 8-26

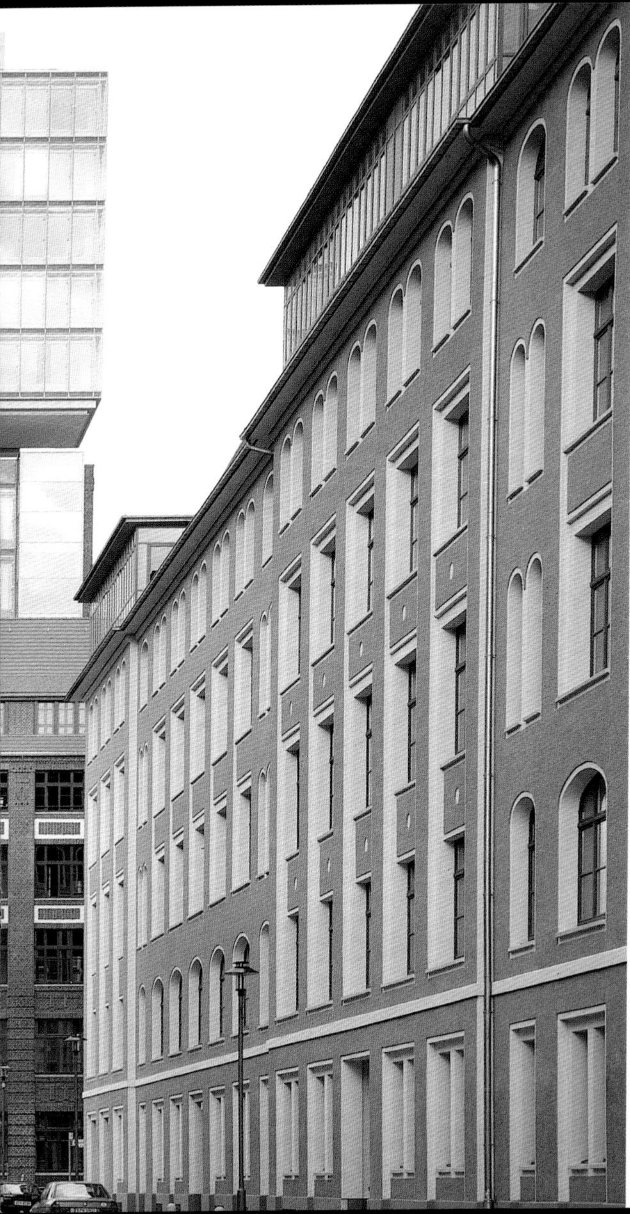

ICC

A great aluminium-clad monument to the era when the car was king in the eyes of town planners, this 1979 conference hall, designed by Ralf Schüler and Ursulina Schüler-Witte, features an eight-lane underground entrance that can process 650 cars in half an hour. Now something of a dinosaur, it was state of the art when built, boasting electronic information boards and 80 halls that can hold 14,500 people. Automated seating folds up to the ceiling to convert Hall 2 into a concert venue. Once one of the largest, most expensive buildings in Germany, it's overshadowed today by multipurpose event spaces, such as O2 World (T 206 070 8899), and will close in 2014 for a three-year, multimillion-euro revamp. *Neue Kantstrasse/Ecke Messedamm, www.icc-berlin.de*

GSW Headquarters

This update of a 1950s Kreuzberg high-rise, with its gentle curves and clever chromatic facade of metal scales, put local architects Sauerbruch Hutton well and truly on the map when it was completed in 1999. The west-facing double-skinned exterior is covered with blinds in white and shades of red, orange and pink, which all open and close independently, regulating the building's heat and light levels and making for a stunning 22-storey piece of abstract art. The structure is best appreciated – in the golden glow of the evening sun – from the lounge of panoramic bar Solar (T 163 765 2700) on nearby Stresemannstrasse.
Charlottenstrasse 4

Kaiser-Wilhelm-Gedächtnis-Kirche

This large, originally unremarkable church, designed by Franz Heinrich Schwechten in 1895, was severely bomb-damaged during WWII. In the 1950s, debate raged about whether to tear it down or rebuild it. The eventual decision, a pioneering one, was to have Berlin's great functionalist architect Egon Eiermann adapt the ruined torso of the tower into a memorial chapel, and build a new church and belltower to go with it. Gabriel Loire's stunning deep-blue windows, flecked with red and gold, help to create a suitably reflective atmosphere in what must be one of the most famous architectural monuments to the futility of war. The church's exterior has been partially wrapped in scaffolding while it is being gradually restored. *Breitscheidplatz, T 218 5023, www.gedaechtniskirche-berlin.de*

Fernsehturm

Berlin's tallest building, a bold 368m spike with a ball in the middle, was conceived by an architects' collective. Based on a 1960s concept by Hermann Henselmann and Jörg Streitparth, the TV Tower is a highlight of the New International architecture around the Alexanderplatz area, much of which has now, sadly, been obscured, 'modernised' or torn down by unappreciative developers. The 1969 Fernsehturm, at least, has remained, and this former symbol of the German Democratic Republic has now become a signature structure of the unified city. The somewhat queasy express lift has been replaced, so – if you can bear the queues – take the 40-second ride 207m up to the rotating Sphere restaurant (T 247 575 875) to drink in the views across Berlin. *Panoramastrasse 1a, www.tv-turm.de*

HOTELS

WHERE TO STAY AND WHICH ROOMS TO BOOK

Berlin is packed with hotels, but only in the late noughties did the more dynamic eastern side of the city finally start to get the properties it deserves. Smartly designed boutique hotels have popped up in and around Mitte, including Casa Camper (see p022) and the adjacent Weinmeister (see p028).

Prices are reasonable for a capital, so it's little wonder that Berlin is still one of Europe's top city-break destinations. However, even the new hotels are more about affordable style than five-star perks. For flawless service look to the Regent (Charlottenstrasse 49, T 20 338) or Hotel Concorde (Augsburger Strasse 41, T 800 9990). If you're visiting during the International Film Festival, a Potsdamer Platz address is a must; try the Grand Hyatt (Marlene-Dietrich-Platz 2, T 2553 1234) and book well ahead. Otherwise head to Tiergarten for Das Stue (see p024) or the Waldorf Astoria (Hardenbergstrasse 28, T 814 0000), opened in 2012 in a Christoph Mäckler-designed skyscraper. A good option for Fashion Week is the stylish Lux 11 (Rosa-Luxemburg-Strasse 9-13, T 936 2800), which has its own designer boutique. Fine alternatives are the Hotel de Rome (see p026) or Cosmo (Spittelmarkt 13, T 5858 2222), designed by SEHW Berlin. Further to the west, the Karl Lagerfeld-decorated Schlosshotel im Grunewald (Brahmsstrasse 10, T 895 840), set in a 1912 mansion, is over-the-top in all the right ways. *For full addresses and room rates, see Resources.*

nhow

Berlin's self-dubbed 'music and lifestyle' hotel, which opened in 2010, sits pretty and pink on the Spree River at the edge of Oberbaum City (see p010). Architect Sergei Tchoban's building may look formal and monolithic from the outside, but its star designer Karim Rashid's biomorphic interiors carry an eye-popping theme throughout, including in the vivid Envy Bar (above). The 304 guest rooms, which follow blue, pink or grey colour schemes, are spacious and futuristic, with curved walls, wave-patterned floors and high-tech sound systems. In keeping with the hotel's musical theme, two state-of-the-art recording studios can be found in nhow's Upper Tower, a mirrored block cantilevered eight storeys over the river. *Stralauer Allee 3, T 290 2990, www.nhow-hotels.com*

Soho House
The London-based members' club and
hotel has dared to take on Berlin with
the renovation of this towering Bauhaus
building. The €40m project, with its
grand accommodations (XL room,
pictured), green-tiled rooftop pool,
private cinema and ubiquitous Cowshed
spa, has become yet another symbol
of the area's continued gentrification.
Torstrasse 1, T 405 0440

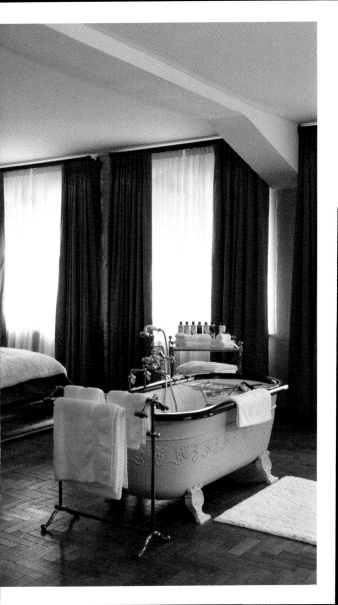

Mani

This 63-room boutique hotel opened in 2012 a few blocks from its big sister, the Amano (T 809 4150), which has been an established stomping ground for Mitte's nightlife gentry since 2009. Mani is smaller, flashier and more sumptuous. Clusters of bamboo and tawny-hued distressed leather reflect off metal and black glass in a lobby replete with a library and photography by Oliver Rath. Rooms are simply divided into two categories, single and double; the latter, including Room 204 (above), are the more spacious. The interiors were designed by local firm Ester Bruzkus Architekten, also responsible for Tim Raue (see p038). The Israeli-French restaurant (opposite; T 016 3635 9464), also called Mani, is likely to be the only spot in town where your foie gras burger includes quince, tahini and black truffle.
Torstrasse 136, T 5302 8080,
www.hotel-mani.com

Casa Camper

This is Camper's second hotel, a zinc-clad building of eight storeys as clever and unpretentious as the brand's shoes. Throughout the accommodation there's a Berlin-inspired flair for the idiosyncratic and dramatic, from the curtain-draped ceiling in the small lobby to the stage-like space of the Asian restaurant, Dos Palillos (T 2000 3413), designed by Ronan and Erwan Bouroullec. However, the 51 identically decorated rooms, which contain African-hardwood floors and light-filled bathrooms, are tranquil rather than striking. We're particularly fond of the roomy Camper Suite (above). The top-floor Tentiempé café provides guests with free drinks and snacks 24-hours a day to go with its views of Berlin. *Weinmeisterstrasse 1, T 2000 3410, www.casacamper.com/berlin*

Michelberger Hotel

If the Michelberger, a quirky flashpacker-style hotel that opened in 2009, feels a bit like a set in an arthouse film, that's because set designer Sibylle Oellerich and actress Anja Knauer helped to dream up the interiors. The ground floor, which comprises a library, a bar and a doughnut-shaped reception area, is a stylish jumble of concrete and wooden floors, cuckoo clocks, mismatching fleamarket chairs, low couches and hanging lamps made from recycled hardcover books. Check into the Loft (above) or one of the four luxury rooms, such as The Chalet, a humorous alpine-style attic with a ceiling of raw wood planks and a red-tiled shower room; or The Golden One, an opulent hideaway where every surface glitters. *Warschauer Strasse 39/40, T 2977 8590, www.michelbergerhotel.com*

Das Stue
First unveiled in 1940 as a Danish embassy designed by architect Johann Emil Schaudt (the man behind the city's premier department store, KaDeWe), this monumental building has stayed true to its classic beginnings. In 2012, it reopened as a hotel, but with an added light-filled trapezoidal wing by architects Axthelm, and striking interiors by Patricia Urquiola. Das Stue, which means 'living room' in Danish, has 80 rooms and suites designed in muted tones by Spanish firm LVG Arquitectura; many have floor-to-ceiling windows overlooking Tiergarten park, and all feature one-off furnishings and Apple entertainment systems. Enjoy avant-garde Mediterranean cuisine by Spanish chef Paco Pérez in the restaurant, Cinco, and drink 'forgotten cocktails' from the 1920s and 1930s in the elegant Stue Bar.
Drakestrasse 1, T 311 7220,
www.das-stue.com

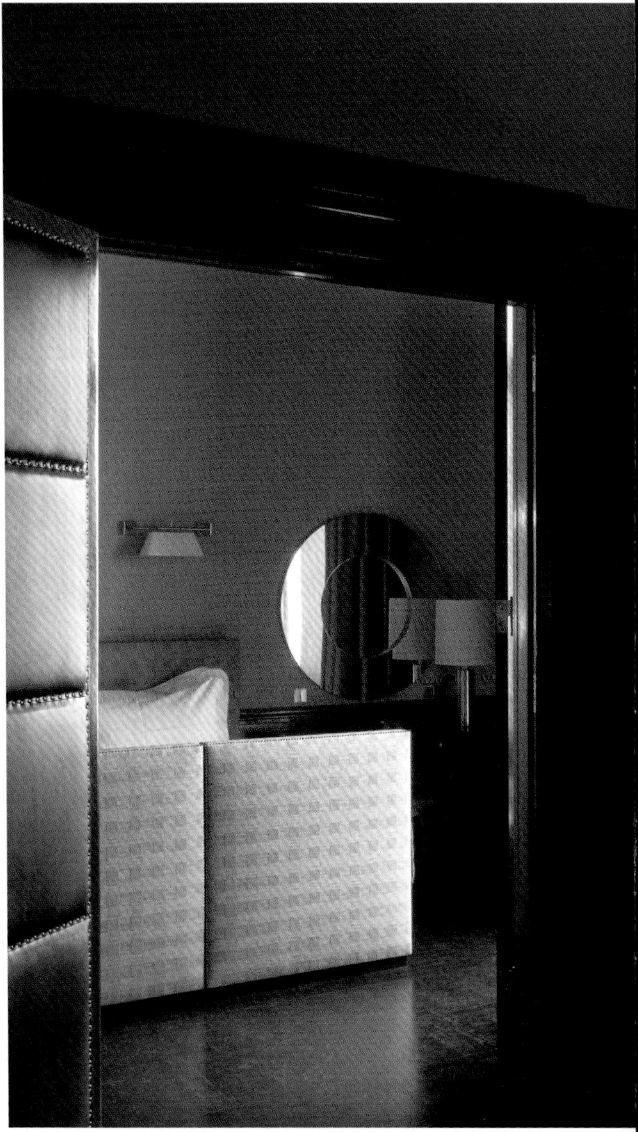

Hotel de Rome
This 1889 building was transformed from a bank into a slick five star in 2006. Book one of the classically proportioned Historic Suites (pictured), which are former directors' offices and feature the original stucco work. Look out for the grenade splinters from WWII still stuck in the wood panelling.
Behrenstrasse 37, T 460 6090, www.hotelderome.com

The Weinmeister

The epicentre of Berlin-Mitte chic, The Weinmeister, which opened in summer 2010, is the consummate style-conscious introduction to the city. Adorning its walls are portraits of the many artists, actors and creative entrepreneurs who frequent the hotel. The British electro-pop band Hurts have their own room, the Hurts Chamber (above), which includes the duo's choice of books, CDs and DVDs alongside an oversized freestanding bed, and an iMac (there's one in each of the 84 rooms). The graffiti-splattered unmarked entrance and the stairwell mural by street-artist collective Paint Club pay tribute to Berlin's reputation as a bohemian playground.
Weinmeisterstrasse 2, T 755 6670, www.the-weinmeister.com

Askanischer Hof

One of the city's best kept secrets, the Askanischer Hof is the *Lieblingshotel* (favourite hotel) of many visiting actors, literary types and photographers. For its spacious old Berlin townhouse style and spotlessly clean rooms at affordable prices, it is unmatched in the city – even if it's a little careworn these days. The art deco lobby and ornate interior detailing recall the original opulence of the building, and the eclectic furnishings span the gamut of 20th-century genres, compiled with an elan that makes location scouts go weak at the knees. Rooms 15 (above) and 16 are impressive examples.
Kurfürstendamm 53, T 881 8033, www.askanischer-hof.de

Hotel-Pension Dittberner

The Main Suite (above) at the 22-room Dittberner, with its Marianne Koplin bedside lamps, raw-silk chaise longue, stucco ceiling and splendid balcony overlooking a quiet street near the Ku'damm, is a lesson in classic West Berlin apartment living. This may only be a pension, but the elegance of the larger rooms beats the pants off most of the big-name hotels, at a fraction of the price. The paintings and sculptures throughout lend artistic flair, and the antique lift, dating to 1911, hints at the history of the place. For a variation on the room service, visit Charlottenburg institution Harry Genenz (T 3377 1977), where you can stock up on *Schwarzwälder kirschtorte* (black forest gâteau). *Wielandstrasse 26, T 884 6950, www.hotel-dittberner.de*

24 HOURS

SEE THE BEST OF THE CITY IN JUST ONE DAY

Berlin is a 24-hour city and only your stamina will tell you when it's time to turn in. The working day begins at 8am and can end as early as 4pm, although creative types tend to keep a 10am-until-late schedule. In summer, weekends start at lunchtime on Fridays, when Berliners throng to outdoor cafés or beer gardens, such as Prater (Kastanienallee 7-9, T 448 5688), which dates to 1837. If you fancy a stroll, Kreuzberg's Gleisdreieck Park (Möckernstrasse), opened in 2013, is worth a visit, as is the Mauerpark weekend fleamarket (Bernauer Strasse 63-64, T 0176 2925 0021).

The art scene is one of Europe's best. Check out Kreuzkölln's nascent gallery district, specifically Crystal Ball (Schönleinstrasse 7, T 6005 2828); or head over to Tiergarten, where you can view exhibitions at the likes of Nolan Judin (Potsdamer Strasse 83, T 3940 4840) or Klosterfelde (Potsdamer Strasse 93, T 283 5305).

There is a bewildering variety of nightlife, from concerts and clubs to the open-air cinemas and canal-side bacchanals that are a Berlin speciality. Look out for flyers or ask the locals. For those who've partied hard, a favoured tonic is a currywurst at Curry36 (Mehringdamm 36, T 251 7368). Opulent breakfasts are served until late in the afternoon at most cafés – try Nola's am Weinberg (Veteranenstrasse 9, T 4404 0766) – so you can grab some food and well-earned sleep before starting all over again.

For full addresses, see Resources.

10.00 Café Einstein

Berliners do *Frühstück* (breakfast) in style, and the original Café Einstein – not to be confused with the venue at Unter den Linden 42 (T 204 3632) – enjoys a great setting and has a traditional feel. Located in an 1878 villa since 1978, it's long been a hangout of the city's bohemians and literati. Order a glass of fresh orange juice, coffee and the Viennese breakfast, which includes fluffy rolls and two peeled soft-boiled eggs in a glass. Add butter and seasoning, gather the day's papers and make the most of the European coffee-house ambience. On warm summer mornings, sit outside in the garden. Upstairs you'll find bar Lebensstern (T 2639 1922), which offers more than 600 types of rum and 150 kinds of gin. *Kurfürstenstrasse 58, T 2639 1921, www.cafeeinstein.com*

12.00 Holocaust Memorial

Nestled between the Brandenburg Gate and Potsdamer Platz is the Memorial to the Murdered Jews of Europe, designed by Peter Eisenman and unveiled in 2005. This impressive monument comprises an undulating field of 2,711 stone monoliths tightly packed into an entire block. You may wonder why Berlin took so long to get round to building it. Yet, when you consider the debate that surrounded the project – from the government rejecting the original designs, to the row about whether it should also honour other Holocaust victims, to the scandal of the contract for the stones' paint being given to a firm whose sister company made the Zyklon B used in the gas chambers – it's a wonder it was ever completed at all. *Cora-Berliner-Strasse 1, T 263 9430, www.holocaust-mahnmal.de*

13.30 Sammlung Boros

Housed inside an imposing bunker, one of Berlin's most intriguing private art collections aligns past and present to phenomenal effect. In a 3,000 sq m space, completed in 1942, contemporary works are displayed in 80 boxy concrete rooms designed to withstand air raids. The building received a makeover in 2008, when advertising mogul Christian Boros installed the highlights of his 700-strong haul of artworks. The current exhibition, 'Boros Collection #2', includes striking pieces by Alicja Kwade, Ai Weiwei and Michael Sailstorfer (*Zeit ist Keine Autobahn*, opposite). Access is only possible via guided tours on Thursdays to Sundays, which are booked through the website. Spots fill up well in advance, so plan ahead.
Reinhardtstrasse 20,
www.sammlung-boros.de

20.00 Tim Raue

Since leaving the Adlon Holding hotel group to launch his eponymous restaurant in 2010, Tim Raue quickly shook up Berlin's fine-dining scene. His daring amalgam of Asian and German cuisine won him a Michelin star three months after opening, and a second in 2013. Set in an old gallery space with high ceilings and poured asphalt floors, the restaurant, designed by local architects Ester Bruzkus and Patrick Batek, pays tribute to its environs in artsy Kreuzberg. Expect flashes of colour and a 'sky' of more than 500 light bulbs above a white marble counter in the bar/lounge. The menu's far-flung influences range from Japanese to Thai, resulting in tantalising oddities such as jasmine pigeon with peanut and fig.
Rudi-Dutschke-Strasse 26, T 2593 7930, www.tim-raue.com

22.00 Prince Charles

Set in a former swimming facility dating to the 1970s, this subterranean club has helped to fuel the resurgence of the Moritzplatz district. The owners – Nicolas Mönch and Wolfgang Farkas – converted the space themselves, preserving the original colourful mosaicked wall in hues of yellow, blue and aquamarine, and developing the venue's interior around it. Come here on the weekend to knock back cocktails with Berlin's hard-partying set in the sunken pool, and dance under a glimmering analogue ceiling installation comprising 600 bulbs that flicker and dim individually. Check the schedule ahead; Prince Charles runs its own literary salon, and if you visit on a weeknight, you might stumble upon a reading in German. *Prinzenstrasse 85f, www.princecharlesberlin.com*

URBAN LIFE

CAFÉS, RESTAURANTS, BARS AND NIGHTCLUBS

Berlin's nocturnal landscape has smartened up over the past few years. The numerous illegal clubs that sprang up in the 1990s – in hard-to-find ruins with little ventilation and few fire exits – have fallen victim to the city's gentrification. In Kreuzberg, clubs are opening inside renovated historic buildings kitted out with high-end sound-systems, examples being Horst Krzbrg (Tempelhofer Ufer 1), Gretchen (Obentrautstrasse 19-21, T 2592 2702) and Chalet (Vor dem Schlesischen Tor 3). But despite the chic aesthetic, there is still an edge to the nightlife. Bar Tausend (see p050), for instance, in the railway arches under Friedrichstrasse S-Bahn, shudders beneath the weight of each passing train.

The culinary scene, too, has improved greatly in recent years. Since opening in 2009, Reinstoff (see p044) has been showered with awards, and Little Otik (Graefestrasse 71, T 5036 2301) has taken organic, locally sourced dining to the next level. Two new hotspots are located inside old schools: Pauly Saal (see p042), in the former Jüdische Mädchenschule (Jewish Girls' School), and The Grand (see p054). Once-gritty Torstrasse is now restaurant row, lined with stylish bistros such as Noto (No 173, T 2009 5387) and 3 Minutes Sur Mer (No 167, T 6730 2052), and clandestine watering holes like Butcher's Bar (No 116, T 6432 8330) – accessed via a telephone booth inside a currywurst joint.

For full addresses, see Resources.

Lokal

At the forefront of Berlin's farm-to-table movement, Lokal, which opened in 2011, is the follow-up to its now defunct but hugely successful predecessor, Kantine, a temporary restaurant in the office space of architect David Chipperfield. At Lokal, Berliner Maren Thimm and her American partner, chef Gary Hoopengardner, serve up regional fare which is bought in from the surrounding areas and forged into a menu that changes daily. Adventurous diners will be pleased by Hoopengardner's fondness for game and innards, which are prepared to perfection. The modern-rustic interior was conceived by local designer Katja Buchholz, and includes handcrafted timber furniture and hanging lamps fashioned from glass fish traps.
Linienstrasse 160, T 2844 9500, www.lokal-berlin.blogspot.com

Pauly Saal

The Judische Mädchenschule – an elegant 1930s five-storey brick school designed by Alexander Beer – was returned to the Jewish community in 2009 and converted to its current incarnation by architects Grüntuch Ernst in 2012. It is now home to three galleries, a museum and three restaurants, including the high-end Pauly Saal in the former gymnasium. The interior is adorned with quirky art pieces, Murano chandeliers and ceramic wall tiles. A large red-and-white missile by Cosima von Bonin is mounted above the open kitchen, where chef Siegfried Danler has been garnering acclaim for his elevated take on regional and seasonal fare. Enjoy dishes such as Pomeranian ox entrecôte or suckling pig and black pudding tortellini.
Auguststrasse 11-13, T 3300 6070, www.paulysaal.com

Reinstoff

Less than a year after opening in 2009, this 35-seat restaurant, set inside a red-brick former fire station and run by chef Daniel Achilles, won a Michelin star. It gained a second in 2011. Achilles divides his edible creations into two menus: 'quite near', comprising regional classics using local ingredients, and 'far away', which is more experimental. The food is presented in an intimate but theatrical setting that plays dramatically with dark and light. Designed by architects Bolwin Wulf, the restaurant uses low-level lighting to accentuate artfully plated dishes, such as halibut poached in verbena oil, whereas the rest of the space remains cloaked in darkness. Reinstoff is open for dinner only, from Tuesday to Saturday. *Edison Höfe, Schlegelstrasse 26c, T 3088 1214, www.reinstoff.eu*

Típica

Until recently, a common complaint in Berlin concerned the scarcity of decent Mexican cuisine. Then, starting with the 2009 opening of Maria Bonita (T 2025 5338), came a new wave of restaurants serving up authentic south-of-the-border grub. Típica is the chicest of the bunch, in a light-filled space designed by architects KLM, who drew on Latin colour schemes with clean white walls and hints of coral and sand. Owner/chef René Brembach had no previous restaurant experience when he launched Típica in 2010, but you wouldn't know it. Try the *tacos al pastor*: grilled pork in a chilli-achiote salsa served in a tortilla. Wash it down with another Mexican original, a sweet hibiscus-infused *agua fresca*.
Rosenstrasse 19, T 2509 9440,
www.tipica.mx

Luzia

Istanbul-bred brothers Kaan and Yasin Müjdeci have helped put a contemporary sheen on Oranienstrasse, Kreuzberg's lived-in boozy strip, with their concept store Voo (see p078) and, a few doors down, the urbane late-night hangout Luzia. Opened in 2007, the bar is popular with twentysomething professionals, savvy tourists and Mitte types in search of debauchery, who pack in nightly between semi-exposed brick walls adorned with gilded mirrors and murals by local street artist Chin Chin. Luzia turns into a bit of a meat market after 1am and is preferable during the day in warmer months, when the floor-to-ceiling glass facade slides away and the outdoor tables are perfect for coffee, cake and people-watching. *Oranienstrasse 34, T 8179 9958, www.luzia.tc*

Alpenstueck
The name translates as 'a piece of the
Alps' and this venue certainly has a
calm, rarefied atmosphere. The pared-
down interior by local firm BFS Design
combines stacked logs with cool grey
tones and balanced lighting. The food
is hearty but contemporary Alpine fare,
made using local produce.
*Gartenstrasse 9, T 2175 1646,
www.alpenstueck.de*

Cantina

In 2009, swanky Bar Tausend (opposite), added a clandestine jewel box of a restaurant, Cantina (above), behind its bar. Heading up the tiny stainless-steel open kitchen is one of Berlin's most creative Asian chefs, Duc Ngo. From his culinary HQ he serves up Latin-Asian-inspired dishes such as Peruvian *tiradito* (similar to ceviche), miso cod, and sashimi salad. There's also a Japanese-influenced cocktail list – try the Oscaland, which blends sake with basil syrup and jasmine tea. Just as appealing is the chance to people-watch. Book a table no earlier than 10pm, as it's after this time that the restaurant starts to heat up with a mix of German art collectors, Russian models and international socialites.
Schiffbauerdamm 11, T 2758 2070, www.tausendberlin.com

Week End

Now an established nightspot, Week End attracts an international crowd. Located in the former Haus des Reisens (see p064), and designed by architects Robertneun, it is a regular venue for vernissages and after-show parties during Fashion Week. Take the rather claustrophobic lift up to the 12th floor and order a drink at the impressive square bar, before making your way over to the adjacent dancefloor, or the one a further three floors up (above). The playlist covers house, techno and electronic, and in true Berlin style, clubbers here tend not to leave any time before 6am. Don't depart without visiting the rooftop terrace, which has low-level seating and views across Alexanderplatz to the sky-piercing Fernsehturm (see p015). *Alexanderstrasse 7, T 2463 1676, www.week-end-berlin.de*

The Grand

Boasting antique paintings, marble floors and leather booths, this restaurant, bar and event space lives up to its name. The building was formerly a school for underprivileged children, dating to 1842, and is now under historic preservation. Interiors mix classicism with some very Berlin touches, including rough walls in fading colours, and a steel chandelier by film-set designer Martina Brünner. In the restaurant (above), chef Tilo Roth specialises in barbecuing fine cuts of meat on a grill that reaches 800°C. The ground-floor bar resembles an explorer's cabinet, featuring animal drawings on the walls and wooden crocodiles in glass cases, and the club DJs play electro and house to a stylish crowd on weekends. *Hirtenstrasse 4, T 278 909 955, www.the-grand-berlin.com*

POP

Formerly known as Flamingo, this hotspot run by party impresario Connie Opper (Berlin Festival), alongside local fashion photographer Florian Kolmer, relaunched in 2013 as POP (Party Obsessed People). Beneath the tracks of the Hackescher Markt S-Bahn station, by the river's edge in Monbijou Park, monied hipsters with elaborate haircuts strut their stuff among semi-ironic 1980s-inflected Palm Beach decor. This is Berlin excess gone commercial, evidenced by some of the city's more expensive cocktails, such as the €8 POP Mojito, embellished with raspberries. Arrive before 11pm if you'd rather not battle your way to the bar.
Kleine Präsidentenstrasse, Monbijou Park

Tin

On a cobbled street overlooking Landwehr canal, Tin (formerly Tin Tin) is a dash of high style in laidback Kreuzkölln. The restaurant and bar's open-plan interior features concrete walls and tables, a hammered-metal counter and dozens of bare light-bulbs, all put together by design firm Karhard, the team behind the interior of Panorama Bar (T 2936 0210). If it sounds a bit grey and heavy, it's not: the ambience is as warm as the friendly service, and as varied as the food. On offer are seasonal and local dishes, which include Caesar salad with strips of lamb, a Kreuzberg-style anchovy platter, and an extensive cocktail list. Tin also opens for lunch in summer, and has a front patio from which diners can observe the paddle boats floating by on the canal.
Paul-Linke-Ufer 39/40, T 4882 6894, www.tin-berlin.com

Paris Bar

This brasserie-style bar and restaurant is a second home for a crowd of local actors and artists, who seem to have been here since it opened in 1962. Owner Michel Würthle originally lined the walls with art by his friend Martin Kippenberger, whose work epitomises the heady days of West Berlin when this was the place to see and be seen. Today his remaining pieces are joined by contributions from the likes of Damien Hirst and Sarah Lucas. Although the in-crowd has mostly moved further east, you may still spot the odd A-lister tucking into a late-night steak here during one of Berlin's annual international events. The food and drinks are decent but not spectacular – but then you come for the clientele, not the cuisine.
Kantstrasse 152, T 313 8052, www.parisbar.net

Borchardt

The social status of being seated at one of the niche tables in Borchardt is not to be underestimated. The restaurant of choice for Berlin's celeb set is not only loved for its *plateaux de fruits de mer* and chilled riesling but also for the fine dramaturgy of its seating allocation: tourists and potential stalkers are placed firmly front of house. Decor follows the style of a classic French brasserie, with marble pillars and golden mosaics. The menu changes daily, but retains a focus on regional dishes, including a lovely Wiener schnitzel and a delicious beef steak with mixed salad, and asparagus is a speciality when it's in season. *Französische Strasse 47, T 8188 6262, www.borchardt-restaurant.de*

Kosmetiksalon Babette
Previously a fashionable GDR cosmetic studio, this 1950s-style bar is the place to start a club crawl – the Marcus Omas Apfelstrudel cocktail is a good choice. During the week, readings and art shows are a regular occurrence, and if your German is up to scratch, take in a film at the Kino International (see p064) nearby. *Karl-Marx-Allee 36, T 0176 3838 8943, www.barbabette.com*

INSIDERS' GUIDE

PHILIPP SCHÖPFER AND DANIEL KLAPSING, DESIGNERS

As the dual founders of design studio 45 Kilo, Philipp Schöpfer (opposite, left) and Daniel Klapsing create custom-made Bauhaus-influenced furniture. Most of their favourite places in Berlin reflect a preference for the pared down. Their drinking den of choice, Buck and Breck (Brunnenstrasse 177), consists of a single room, almost entirely taken up by a counter, around which guests sip cocktails. 'You have to ring the bell to get in,' explains Schöpfer. For inspiration, they head to Johann König (Dessauer Strasse 6-7, T 2610 3080), a 'huge space that offers artists the ability to show large installations', or Appel Design Galerie (Torstrasse 114, T 3251 8160), which specialises in midcentury furniture. 'There aren't many design galleries that have a gallery atmosphere,' observes Klapsing. 'Here, it's nothing more than the actual pieces.'

Fans of Mitte's independent retail scene, the pair shop at Soto (Torstrasse 72, T 2576 2070), a men's concept store stocking labels such as Our Legacy, and Marron (Augustrasse 77-78, T 2809 4878), a furniture, design and accessories boutique. Both also relish trips to the ramen restaurant Cocolo (Gipsstrasse 3). When it comes to clubbing, instead of queuing to get into techno temple Berghain (Wriezener Bahnhof, T 2936 0210), they hit the venue at 5pm on Sunday. 'Looking at all the people who stayed for two nights in a row is quite interesting, and a little embarrassing,' says Schöpfer. _For full addresses, see Resources._

ARCHITOUR

A GUIDE TO BERLIN'S ICONIC BUILDINGS

You can't beat Berlin for its panoply of 20th-century architecture, from Bauhaus to new brutalist, with all shades of ugly, charming and ridiculous in-between. Its many architectural showpieces include Hans Scharoun's Philharmonie (Herbert-von-Karajan-Strasse 1, T 2548 8999); Foster + Partners' revamped Reichstag (Platz der Republik 1, T 2273 2152); Daniel Libeskind's dramatic Jewish Museum (Lindenstrasse 9-14, T 2599 3300), to which the architect added an education centre in 2012; Mies van der Rohe's Neue Nationalgalerie (Potsdamer Strasse 50, T 266 424 242); and the Fernsehturm (see p015). Berlin has so many gems, from Peter Behrens' AEG Turbine Factory (Huttenstrasse 12-19) to Foster + Partners' Philological Library (Habelschwerdter Allee 45, T 8385 8888), that we can only list the highlights of the highlights.

Although the city was reunified more than 20 years ago, it's still intriguing to compare GDR and FRG architecture. For example, the Stalinist Karl-Marx-Allee, which leads to Hermann Henselmann's Internationalist buildings – encompassing the Haus des Reisens (Alexanderplatz 7), and Kino International (Karl-Marx-Allee 33, T 2475 6011) – contrasts with the Western equivalent, the less bombastic but still inspiring structures of the 1957 International Building Exhibition (Interbau) in Hansaviertel, which includes work by Oscar Niemeyer, Walter Gropius and Werner Düttmann. *For full addresses, see Resources.*

KOW

Initially gentrified when young galleries sprung up hawking edgy emerging art, gritty Brunnenstrasse is now crammed with fun independent boutiques. Holding strong as the street's artistic centrepiece, however, is architect Arno Brandlhuber's sharp minimalist building. Sitting between a pair of old townhouses, the five-storey structure has an opaque white jagged facade that glows at night. Brandlhuber,

who lives in the penthouse and has a studio on the floor below, shares this modernist space with *032c* magazine. Also resident is the fascinating Koch Oberhuber Wolff (KOW), a gallery whose largely academic and political aesthetic was established in 2008 by three curators: Alexander Koch, Nikolaus Oberhuber and Jocelyn Wolff. *Brunnenstrasse 9, T 3116 6770, www.kow-berlin.com*

Haus der Kulturen der Welt
Designed by the US architect Hugh
Stubbins and completed in 1957, this
former conference centre is known
as the 'pregnant oyster' because of its
shell-shaped concrete roof. Restored
in 2007, it's now a contemporary arts
space. The pool outside is home to a
1984 Henry Moore bronze, *Big Butterfly*.
John-Foster-Dulles-Allee 10,
T 3978 7175, www.hkw.de

DZ Bank Building

Restrained by strict building regulations in a historically sensitive location on Pariser Platz, between the Hotel Adlon Kempinski and the Brandenburg Gate, Frank Gehry's first building in Berlin saves its deconstructivist surprises for the interior. Finished in 2001, the deceptively plain limestone facade of the former DG Bank gives way to a writhing fish-like form (a common inspiration for Gehry) in glass, wood and metal that dominates the central atrium (above). The shiny, curvaceous belly of the 'whale' houses the AXICA conference hall, part of what is now an office and residential block. *Pariser Platz 3*

Neues Museum

Closed for 70 years after being bombed during WWII, the Neues Museum finally reopened, after much effort and €233m-worth of funding, to great fanfare in 2009. And although the iconic 'Bust of Nefertiti' is still drawing crowds, it is the building's clever renovation by British architect David Chipperfield that has satisfied critics. Chipperfield and his team did not simply reconstruct what was here or clean up the fragments, they created rooms where one can still see and feel Friedrich August Stüler's original design. Where elements had to be replaced, like the main stairway, Chipperfield rebuilt the original but used different materials, such as pre-cast concrete, to give the space both a modern look and a ghostly feel.
Bodestrasse 1-3, T 266 424 242,
www.neues-museum.de

Labels 2

The city has started to augment the banks of the meandering Spree River, slowly lining it with architectural jewels. One such example is the showy Labels 2, designed by Swiss architects HHF and opened in 2010. Behind the wave-patterned concrete facade, inspired by the Spree and by the arched windows of a neighbouring warehouse, lies a complex of fashion showrooms and event spaces (Berlin is attempting to bring international attention to its youthful and innovative fashion scene). Also of interest is the structure's clever eco-friendly design. The building was constructed with a network of tubes that contain water from the river, heated during winter and cooled during summer. This fluid system reduces Labels 2's energy consumption by an impressive 40 per cent.
Stralauer Allee 12, T 8906 4210

SHOPPING

THE BEST RETAIL THERAPY AND WHAT TO BUY

The Scheunenviertel area offers a host of independent boutiques centred around Neue Strasse and Alte Schönhauser Strasse. Try not to leave out any side streets, as even the smallest hide real gems. Mulackstrasse is fertile ground for up-and-coming retailers so shop for womenswear at Schwarzhogerzeil (No 28, T 2887 3868), stationery at RSVP (No 14, T 2809 4644) and accessories at Hecking (Gormannstrasse 8-9, T 2804 7528). Concept stores like Andreas Murkudis (see p074) and Happy Shop (Torstrasse 67 T 2900 9501), are popular, or visit independent labels Adddress (Weinmeisterstrasse 12-14, T 2887 3434) and Anuschka Hoevener (Linienstrasse 196, T 4431 9299) to stock up on unique pieces Some notable shops can also be found in Charlottenburg: P&T (Bleibtreustrasse 4, T 9561 5468) sells rare teas in a stylish setting

When searching for big-brand fashion, there are two major drags to explore. Out west, along Kurfürstendamm, Jil Sander (No 185, T 886 7020) sits alongside other global brands, while in Schöneberg is the grand dame KaDeWe (Tauentzienstrasse 21-24 T 21 210). Friedrichstrasse, in the former East, is home to Galeries Lafayette (No 76-78, T 209 480) and the elegant covered arcade Quartier 206 (No 71, T 2094 6500), which contains the pioneering concept emporium Departmentstore Quartier 206, designed by the local style guru Anne Maria Jagdfeld.

For full addresses, see Resources.

Objets Trouvés

A stockist of industrial design and vintage furniture, Objets Trouvés built on the success of its original Prenzlauer Berg store (now closed) and opened this outlet in Scheunenviertel in 2011. The name translates as 'found objects', and owners Magdalena and Robert Hohberg travel across Europe searching for pieces that seem to tell a story. Highlights include wood-and-glass medicine cabinets from the 1920s, original Egon Eiermann and Harry Bertoia chairs, and timber benches from Prague topped with cognac-coloured leather. The space itself, with its slate-hued tile flooring and windowed facade, was once a GDR-era cinema, and you can still see the opening on the back wall of the shop, through which the projector shone. *Rosenthaler Strasse 71, T 016 3181 0985, www.objets-trouves-berlin.de*

Andreas Murkudis

Although Mitte is still ground zero for high-end boutique shopping, the 2011 opening of Andreas Murkudis' unisex fashion emporium on the resurgent Potsdamer Strasse has given Berlin's style-set ample occasion to head west. Murkudis elicited the assistance of local architects Gonzalez Haase to fill his new 1,000 sq m digs – housed in a former newspaper printing press – home to a carefully curated but diverse range of items, from Margiela ankle boots to Nymphenburg porcelain and scarves by Neri Firenze. Exhibitions are sometimes held, local sunglasses firm Mykita has its own concession, and there's a sunken level in which furniture by German brand e15 is sold. Closed Sundays.
Potsdamer Strasse 81e, T 680 798 306, www.andreasmurkudis.com

Lunettes Selection

In 2006, frustrated by the difficulty of finding stylish vintage eyewear in the city, Uta Geyer decided to launch her own boutique, Lunettes, in Prenzlauer Berg (T 4373 9465). A second outlet on Torstrasse opened in 2010, and the understated shop carries an excellent crop of classic frames by brands such as Ray-Ban, Algha and Cazal, which are kept in a large 1950s wooden commode.

Directly across from it, an old-school eye-test chart hangs on the white wall. In 2010, Geyer launched the Lunettes Kollektion, a line of vintage-influenced specs, which includes the 'Jean Claude' (above), €259. These are all handmade in Italy and sold in cases inspired by 1920s soap and chocolate boxes.
Torstrasse 172, T 2021 5216,
www.lunettes-selection.com

Voo Store

Located within a former locksmiths in a *Hinterhof* (back courtyard) on Kreuzberg's still gritty Oranienstrasse, Voo combines hipster street style with sustainability and a preference for small, cutting-edge manufacturers. Opened in 2010, it hosts brands such as Acne, Carin Wester and local label Don't Shoot the Messengers, as well as selling surprising one-off items like Hudsalva, the lip balm of the Swedish military. There's a set of turntables for DJs to spin, and owners Yasin and Kaan Müjdeci, of bar Luzia (see p046), utilise the shop as a venue for exhibitions, readings and live concerts. In 2013, Voo unveiled another draw – Shawn Barber and Christoph Onton's on-site café, Companion Coffee (T 176 6344 6225). *Oranienstrasse 24, T 6165 1119, www.vooberlin.com*

The Corner Berlin

A temple to good taste on the corner of the elegant Gendarmenmarkt square, The Corner Berlin is co-owned by Josef Voelk and Emmanuel De Bayser. Its simple white-and-brown interior, designed by Gonzalez Haase, is offset by an excellent selection of covetable items, including men's and women's fashion from the likes of Saint Laurent Paris, Balenciaga and Alexander McQueen, as well as furniture, design pieces and art books. A second branch (T 8892 1261) opened in 2012, as did a men's store in Mitte (T 2061 3764). Both were done out by Voelk and De Bayser with the assistance of interior designer Johann Alexander Stütz. *Französische Strasse 40, T 2067 0940, www.thecornerberlin.de*

Sprüth Magers
This sprawling gallery, set in a former
dance hall, was opened by art-world
figures Monika Sprüth and Philomene
Magers in 2008. Artists such as Andrea
Zittel ('Pattern of Habit', pictured), Cindy
Sherman and Andreas Gursky continue
to exhibit, and the venue also has a DVD
shop, Image Movement, which screens
art films on a regular basis.
Oranienburger Strasse 18, T 2888 4030

MDC Cosmetic

Opened in 2012, this airy boutique offers a unique range of cosmetics and toiletries made by small-scale brands from around the world. Owner Melanie dal Canton, who cut her teeth as a manager at Andreas Murkudis (see p074), has lovingly curated the unisex selection. Here you'll find retro-packaged toothpaste from the historic Portuguese brand Couto alongside natural mouthwash made by German label Apomanum (above), €9.95, and elegant, hammered-silver soap dishes share shelving with cashmere-covered hot-water bottles. The space, again the work of Gonzalez Haase, looks on to one of Prenzlauer Berg's most idyllic squares. Treatments, such as facials, manicures and pedicures are offered in a back room. *Knaackstrasse 26, T 4005 6339, www.mdc-cosmetic.com*

Gestalten

In 2011, Gestalten, a Berlin-based design, art and architecture publisher, opened a shop-cum-gallery in an artsy courtyard complex that's long been an institution in the area. In this vast 350 sq m showroom with original features, such as wood floors and vaulted ceilings, Gestalten showcases its entire catalogue in a space designed by the company's own team. All 400-plus of the publisher's books, including hard- to-find archive titles, are for sale, as are toys and homewares by the likes of Marcel Wanders. There is also a gallery area for temporary shows, which have included collaborations with local conceptual product designers Beta Tank. *Sophie-Gips-Höfe, Sophienstrasse 21, T 2021 5821, www.gestalten.com*

Apartment

To find this subterranean, cutting-edge fashion boutique you have to enter an unmarked door, go through an empty, all-white storefront and then down a dark spiral staircase. Finally, you arrive in a cave-like narrow space, lit with bars of fluorescent light, displaying a mix of rather well-edited cultish fashion items for men and women, including a sleeveless shield jacket by Rick Owens. We've also heard that you can bargain with the salespeople here, but for more friendly Berlin-style price points, head next door to the store's design outlet, Cash. *Memhardstrasse 8, T 2804 2251, www.apartmentberlin.de*

SPORTS AND SPAS
WORK OUT, CHILL OUT OR JUST WATCH

Being flat, Berlin is a haven for cycling, and an extensive network of paths makes this the perfect way to get around town. In the summer, the city is dotted with Deutsche Bahn's distinctive hire bikes (T 0700 0522 5522, www.callabike-interaktiv.de), which you can pick up and ride, using your mobile phone to pay.

Per capita, Berlin has a high proportion of public swimming pools, including some of the most well-designed and equipped in Europe. Opening times, however, are at best erratic and at worst annoying. Ask your concierge to investigate. Otherwise, the clean lakes surrounding the city offer bathing and sailing in summer or skating in winter. The Olympiastadion (opposite), built for the 1936 Games, is an impressive venue, and it is worth buying tickets to see the local football team, Hertha (www.herthabsc.de).

Most spas, or 'wellness' areas, are in the main hotels; the super Spa de Rome (T 460 609 1160) at Hotel de Rome (see p026), for example. Or check into Aveda Hairspa (T 2809 1918) at the Lux 11 (see p016), or the Club Olympus Fitness Centre & Spa in the Grand Hyatt (see p016). When Das Stue (see p024) opened, it launched the Susanne Kaufmann Spa, offering an indoor pool, a sauna and treatments influenced by traditional Chinese medicine. For an experience you won't forget, try Viktor Leske (Lausitzer Platz 1 T 6003 1562), a high-end salon in a former tunnel.

For full addresses, see Resources.

Olympiastadion

This iconic oval structure, designed by Werner March, may owe its external form to its National Socialist past, but inside it is a superb example of modern stadium design. Initially built as the main venue for the 1936 Olympics, it was renovated between 2000 and 2004 by Hamburg architects von Gerkan, Marg und Partner (GMP) in preparation for hosting the 2006 FIFA World Cup Final. The limestone facade is deceptive; the interior is scooped out and more than half the stadium lies underground. GMP lowered the pitch by a further 2.65m to increase the seating capacity to 74,244, and added a delicate, translucent roof membrane, which slots seamlessly into the original structure. Check out the view from the 77m belltower. *Olympischer Platz 3, T 3068 8100, www.olympiastadion-berlin.de*

Velodrom
French architect Dominique Perrault's circular indoor velodrome opened in 1997 and nestles mostly below ground under a shimmering metal roof. Capable of holding 12,000 spectators, it is used more for concerts than cycling. Head next door to see the equally stylish pool complex, one of the largest in Europe. *Paul-Heyse-Strasse 26, T 443 045, www.velodrom.de*

Schon geduscht?

Liquidrom

Berlin's clubbiest spa allows guests to listen to electronic or classical music, performed live or selected by DJs, while floating in a warm, darkened 'sound pool' surrounded by colourful light projections (opposite). The stylish complex, which has airy relaxation rooms and a dome-shaped inner sanctum, is the work of GMP, who also designed Berlin's Hauptbahnhof (see p009). Four types of massage are offered, including a Balinese herbal ball treatment, and there are three saunas, three pools (including a plunge pool, above) and a steam bath. The crowd is an interesting mix: in the Japanese onsen pool or Himalaya salt sauna, expect to see couples next to hungover folks who've clearly arrived straight from the dancefloor. *Möckernstrasse 10, T 258 007 820, www.liquidrom-berlin.de*

Badeschiff

What started off as an urban-regeneration experiment to enliven Berlin's neglected river area turned into one of the city's favourite R&R venues. Opened in 2004, the Badeschiff (bathing ship) is essentially an old barge on the Spree that was refitted as a heated pool by Spanish firm AMP in collaboration with local architect Gil Wilk and artist Susanne Lorenz. The wood decking and docklands ambience, as well as the regular events and DJs, make it a perfect post-industrial venue for a lazy afternoon, particularly in the height of summer. During the winter, cocoon-like coverings (above) ensure that the pool, bar, sauna and massage area are kept at a cosy temperature, in direct contrast to the ice-floe-filled river on which they sit. *Eichenstrasse 4, T 533 2030, www.badeschiff.de*

ESCAPES

WHERE TO GO IF YOU WANT TO LEAVE TOWN

It's hard to run out of things to do in Berlin, but if you do need respite from the city, you can take a train to almost anywhere in Europe from the Hauptbahnhof (see p009). Szczecin in Poland is only 140km away and is a popular day trip, but you don't have to cross the border – options include Hamburg (90 minutes via the high-speed link), Leipzig (just over an hour) and Dresden (about two hours). A visit to Dessau (opposite) is an inspiring journey back to the engine room of the Bauhaus movement. The sandy-shored lakes on the city's outskirts and in surrounding Brandenburg are perfect for nature lovers. In summer, Wannsee Strandbad (see p100), and Werbellinsee, an hour north, are lovely, and in winter, packing a hot toddy and going ice-skating there is a great day out.

Potsdam, the former summer residence of the Hohenzollerns, was wrecked by WWII and East German road planners, but it's now a well-restored, pretty town, located 25km south-west of Berlin. In summer, the crowds at Sanssouci Palace (Maulbeerallee, T 033 1969 4200) are a drag, but Erich Mendelsohn's expressionist Einsteinturm (see p101) justifies the pilgrimage and the trek through the Albert Einstein Science Park. Also worth seeking out in Potsdam is Rudy Ricciotti's interior for the Nikolaisaal concert hall (Wilhelm-Staab-Strasse 10-11, T 033 1288 8828), a rare piece of contemporary architecture hidden behind a baroque facade. *For full addresses, see Resources.*

Bauhaus Building, Dessau

Only an hour and a half from Berlin, this design site is an essential destination for modernism fans. Dessau was the home of the Bauhaus movement between 1925 and 1932, and founder Walter Gropius' building rapidly became an iconic structure. The architecture and its historical significance motivated UNESCO to add the Bauhaus Building and the nearby Masters' Houses to its World Heritage list in 1996. You can book twice-daily tours (in German only) to see the interiors, including the auditorium and the director's room. Of the remaining Masters' Houses, both Oskar Schlemmer's former residence (T 034 0650 8303) and the beautifully restored living quarters of Paul Klee and Wassily Kandinsky (overleaf; T 034 0661 0934) are essential viewing. *Gropiusallee 38, T 034 0650 8250, www.bauhaus-dessau.de*

Kandinsky/Klee House, Dessau

Wannsee Strandbad

If you have a hankering for messing about in boats, you don't have to travel far out of Berlin. The Wannsee is a lake complex surrounded by forest, connected to the city's second-largest river, the Havel. It is located south-west of Berlin near Potsdam, about half an hour away by train. Wannsee Strandbad is one of the longest inland lidos in Europe, with a beach stretching 1,275m along the shore. Here you can hire rowing boats or just kick back on one of the distinctive wicker chairs (above), which can be rented for €8 a day. The beach itself can get crowded; sailing is more relaxing but you'll need to befriend a local with a yacht or talk to your concierge.

Einsteinturm, Potsdam

This curious tower, completed in 1921, was designed by Erich Mendelsohn for the astronomer Erwin Finlay-Freundlich to observe the sun and to substantiate Einstein's Theory of Relativity. Legend has it that Mendelsohn took Einstein on a tour of the tower to get his impression. The physicist's one-word review was 'organic'. In fact, the building was so experimental that it only remains in place thanks to constant renovation work, as the early concrete from which it was built is not up to the structural task, so visit before gravity gets the upper hand. Afterwards, make your way to Restaurant Juliette (T 033 1270 1791) in Potsdam's Dutch quarter to enjoy classic French fare in comfortable surroundings.
Albert Einstein Science Park, Telegrafenberg, T 033 174 990, www.aip.de

GfZK, Leipzig
The city of Leipzig in Saxony has a cultural tradition encompassing art, book fairs, education and JS Bach. Its politically minded GfZK (gallery of contemporary art) puts on exhibitions and funds projects that aim to examine the role of art in a post-socialist country. The café/bar is lively both day and night.
Karl-Tauchnitz-Strasse 9-11,
T 034 114 0810, www.gfzk.de

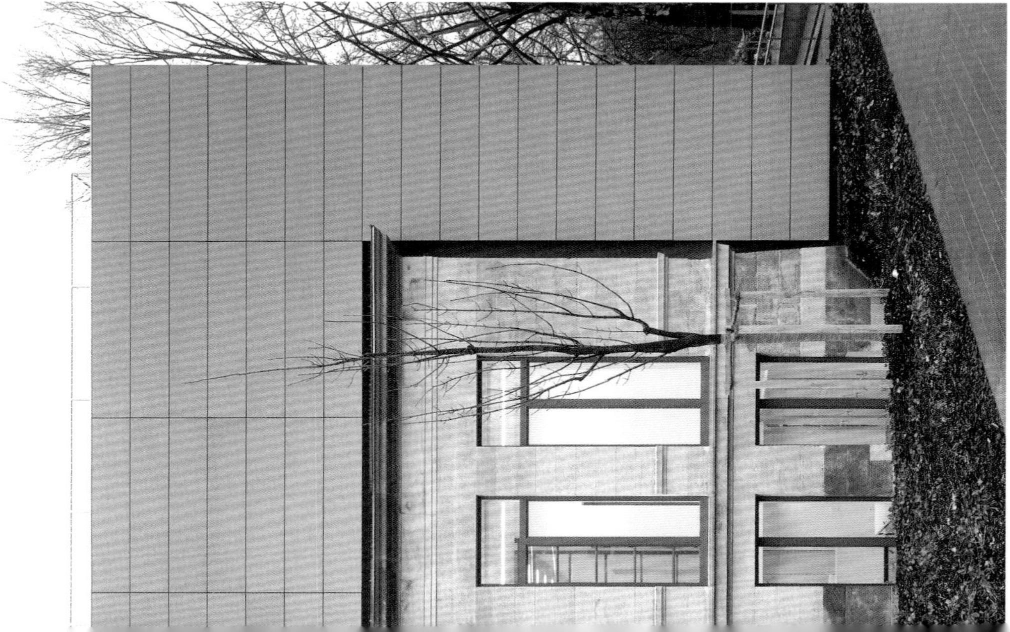

NOTES

SKETCHES AND MEMOS

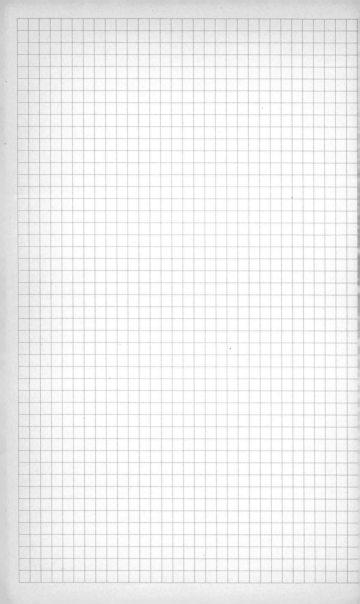

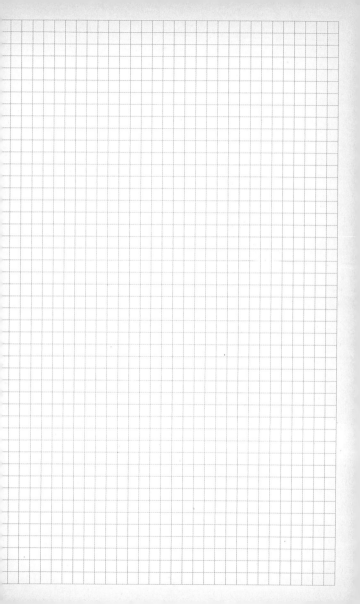

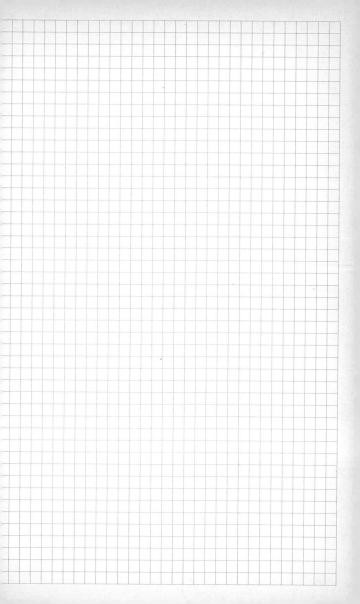

RESOURCES

CITY GUIDE DIRECTORY

HOTELS
ADDRESSES AND ROOM RATES

Hotel Amano 020
Room rates:
double, from €85
Augustrasse 43
T 809 4150
www.hotel-amano.com

Askanischer Hof 029
Room rates:
double, from €120;
Room 15, from €145;
Room 16, from €150
Kurfürstendamm 53
T 881 8033
www.askanischer-hof.de

Casa Camper 022
Room rates:
double, from €195;
Camper Suite, from €340
Weinmeisterstrasse 1
T 2000 3410
www.casacamper.com/berlin

Hotel Concorde 016
Room rates:
double, from €130
Augsburger Strasse 41
T 800 9990
www.hotelconcordeberlin.com

Cosmo 016
Room rates:
double, from €105
Spittelmarkt 13
T 5858 2222
www.cosmo-hotel.de

Hotel-Pension Dittberner 030
Room rates:
double, from €90;
Main Suite, €140
Wielandstrasse 26
T 884 6950
www.hotel-dittberner.de

Grand Hyatt 016
Room rates:
double, from €250
Marlene-Dietrich-Platz 2
T 2553 1234
www.berlin.grand.hyatt.de

Lux 11 016
Room rates:
double, from €80
Rosa-Luxemburg-Strasse 9-13
T 936 2800
www.lux-eleven.com

Mani 020
Room rates:
double, from €75;
Room 204, from €75
Torstrasse 136
T 5302 8080
www.hotel-mani.com

Michelberger Hotel 023
Room rates:
double, from €60;
Loft, from €80;
The Chalet, from €140;
The Golden One, from €140
Warschauer Strasse 39/40
T 2977 8590
www.michelbergerhotel.com

nhow 017
Room rates:
double, from €115
Stralauer Allee 3
T 290 2990
www.nhow-hotels.com

Regent 016
Room rates:
double, from €215
Charlottenstrasse 49
T 20 338
www.theregentberlin.com

Hotel de Rome 026
Room rates:
double, from €245;
Historic Suite, €2,600
Behrenstrasse 37
T 460 6090
www.hotelderome.com

Schlosshotel im Grunewald 016
Room rates:
double, from €240
Brahmsstrasse 10
T 895 840
www.schlosshotelberlin.com

Soho House 018
Room rates:
double, from €110;
XL, €800
Torstrasse 1
T 405 0440
www.sohohouseberlin.com

Das Stue 024
Room rates:
double, from €180
Drakestrasse 1
T 311 7220
www.das-stue.com

Waldorf Astoria 016
Room rates:
double, from €210
Hardenbergstrasse 28
T 814 0000
www.waldorfastoriaberlin.com

The Weinmeister 028
Room rates:
double, from €100;
Hurts Chamber, €350
Weinmeisterstrasse 2
T 755 6670
www.the-weinmeister.com

WALLPAPER* CITY GUIDES

Executive Editor
Rachael Moloney

Editor
Ella Marshall

Authors
Kimberly Bradley
Rachel B Doyle
Charly Wilder

Art Director
Loran Stosskopf

Art Editor
Eriko Shimazaki

Designer
Mayumi Hashimoto

Map Illustrator
Russell Bell

Photography Editor
Elisa Merlo

Assistant Photography Editor
Nabil Butt

Chief Sub-Editor
Nick Mee

Sub-Editor
Farah Shafiq

Editorial Assistant
Emma Harrison

Interns
Romy van den Broeke
Phil James

Wallpaper* Group Editor-in-Chief
Tony Chambers

Publishing Director
Gord Ray

Managing Editor
Oliver Adamson

Contributors
Joanna Kornacki
Sophie Lovell
Gisella Williams

Wallpaper* ® is a registered trademark of IPC Media Limited

First published 2007
Revised and updated 2009, 2010, 2011, 2012 and 2013

All prices are correct at the time of going to press, but are subject to change.

Printed in China

PHAIDON

Phaidon Press Limited
Regent's Wharf
All Saints Street
London N1 9PA

Phaidon Press Inc
180 Varick Street
New York, NY 10014

Phaidon® is a registered trademark of Phaidon Press Limited

www.phaidon.com

A CIP Catalogue record for this book is available from the British Library.

ISBN 978 0 7148 6611 6

PHOTOGRAPHERS

Bildarchiv Monheim GmbH/Alamy
Einsteinturm, p101

Benjamin Blossom
Hotel de Rome, pp026-027
Kosmetiksalon Babette, pp060-061
Haus der Kulturen der Welt, pp066-067
Olympiastadion, p089
Badeschiff, pp094-095

Bitter Bredt
GSW Headquarters, p013

Martin Brück
Bauhaus Building, p097

Roderick Coyne
Kandinsky/Klee House, pp098-099

Michael Danner
Kaiser-Wilhelm-Gedächtnis-Kirche, p014
Casa Camper, p022
Michelberger Hotel, p023
Reinstoff, p044
Cantina, p051
Neues Museum, p069
Labels 2, pp070-071
Apartment, p085

Diephotodesigner.de
Berlin city view, inside front cover
Askanischer Hof, p029
Hotel-Pension Dittberner, pp030-031
Café Einstein, p033
Paris Bar, p058
Borchardt, p059
DZ Bank Building, p068

Georges Fessy
Velodrom, pp090-091

Michael Franke
Holocaust Memorial, pp034-035
Pauly Saal, pp042-043
The Grand, p054
Philipp Schöpfer and Daniel Klapsing, p063
MDC Cosmetic, p082
Liquidrom, p092, p093

Marcus Gaab
Soho House, pp018-019

Sabine Götz
Wannsee Strandbad, p100

Frank Herfort
Mani, p020, p021
Lokal, p041
Típica, p045
Luzia, p046, p047
POP, p055

Objets Trouvés, p073
Andreas Murkudis, pp074-075
Lunettes Selection, p076
Voo Store, p078

Nagib Khazaka
nhow, p017
The Weinmeister, p028
Tin, pp056-057
Gestalten, p084

Noshe
ICC, p012
Sammlung Boros, p036, p037
KOW, p065

Peartree Digital
Lunettes frames, p077
MDC mouthwash, p083

Patrick Voigt
Fernsehturm, p015

Jens Ziehe/Courtesy the artist and Sprüth Magers Berlin London
Sprüth Magers, pp080-081

BERLIN
A COLOUR-CODED GUIDE TO THE HOT 'HOODS

TIERGARTEN
Many of Berlin's most remarkable buildings are in and around its central green space

SCHEUNENVIERTEL
Explore beyond the tourist thoroughfares to discover this area's intriguing boutiques

KREUZBERG
Still edgy and filled with creatives and hip eateries, this is the city's cultural melting pot

FRIEDRICHSHAIN
Communist architecture lines the main roads here and side streets offer many surprises

CHARLOTTENBURG
The capital's main shopping drag is a draw, as are the upmarket restaurants and hotels

MITTE
Bomb damage has been replaced by exciting new architecture in the city's centre

PRENZLAUER BERG
This district is known for its 19th-century apartment buildings and Sunday-brunch venues

SCHÖNEBERG
Leafy boulevards and grand villas fill the old West, stretching as far as the Wannsee lakes

For a full description of each neighbourhood, see the Introduction.
Featured venues are colour-coded, according to the district in which they are located.